Android Interview Questions and Answers

1. What is android?

A.Android is a stack of software for mobile devices which has Operating System, middleware and some key applications. The application executes within its own process and its own instance of Dalvik Virtual Machine. Many Virtual Machines run efficiently by a DVM device. DVM executes Java language byte code which later transforms into .dex format files.

2. What are the advantages of Android?

A. The following are the advantages of Android:

* The customer will be benefited from wide range of mobile applications to choose, since the monopoly of wireless carriers like AT&T and Orange will be broken by Google Android.
* Features like weather details, live RSS feeds, opening screen, icon on the opening screen can be customized
* Innovative products like the location-aware services, location of a nearby convenience store etc., are some of the additive facilities in Android.
   Components can be reused and replaced by the application framework.
* Optimized DVM for mobile devices
* SQLite enables to store the data in a structured manner.
* Supports GSM telephone and Bluetooth, WiFi, 3G and EDGE technologies
* The development is a combination of a device emulator, debugging tools, memory profiling and plug-in for Eclipse IDE.

3. Explain about the exceptions of Android?

A.The following are the exceptions that are supported by Android
* InflateException : When an error conditions are occurred, this exception is thrown
* Surface.OutOfResourceException: When a surface is not created or resized, this exception is thrown
* SurfaceHolder.BadSurfaceTypeException: This exception is thrown from the lockCanvas() method, when invoked on a Surface whose is SURFACE_TYPE_PUSH_BUFFERS
* WindowManager.BadTokenException: This exception is thrown at the time of trying to add view an invalid WindowManager.LayoutParamstoken.

4. Describe the APK format.

A.The APK file is compressed the AndroidManifest.xml file, application code (.dex files), resource files, and other files. A project is compiled into a single .apk file.

5. What is .apk extension?

A.The extension for an Android package file, which typically contains all of the files related to a single Android application. The file itself is a compressed collection of an AndroidManifest.xml file, application code (.dex files), resource files, and other files. A project is compiled into a single .apk file.

6. What is .dex extension?

A.Android programs are compiled into .dex (Dalvik Executable) files, which are in turn zipped into a single .apk file on the device. .dex files can be created by automatically translating compiled applications written in the Java programming language.

7. Explain the Architecture of Android ?

A. Top -> Applications (Contacts, Browser, Phone, etc)

Below Applications -> Application Framework(Activity Manager, Window Manager, Content Providers, View System, Package manager,

Telephony manager, Resource, Notification, Location managers)

Below Application Framework -> System Libraries(Like Sqlite, webkit, SSL, OpenGL, Media Framework etc) & Android Runtime(Core Libraries and DVM).

Atlast Last -> Linux Kernel (which composed of drivers like display, camera etc.)

10. What is an activity?

A. A single screen in an application, with supporting Java code.

An activity presents a visual user interface for one focused endeavor the user can undertake.

For example, an activity might present a list of menu items users can choose from or it might display photographs along with their captions.

11. What is a service?

A.A service doesn't have a visual user interface, but rather runs in the background for an indefinite period of time.

For example, a service might play background music as the user attends to other matters, or it might fetch data over the network or calculate something and provide the result to activities that need it.Each service extends the Service base class.

12. How to Remove Desktop icons and Widgets?

A. Press and Hold the icon or widget. The phone will vibrate and on the bottom of the phone you will see anoption to remove. While still holding the icon or widget drag it to the remove button. Once remove turns red drop the item and it is gone

13. Describe a real time scenario where android can be used?

A . Imagine a situation that you are in a country where no one understands the language you speak and you can not read or write. However, you have mobile phone with you.

14. How to select more than one option from list in android xml file? ********

A. Give an example.
Specify android id, layout height and width as depicted in the following example.

15. What languages does Android support for application development?

A.Android applications are written using the Java programming language.

16. Describe Android Application Architecture?

A.Android Application Architecture has the following components:

• Services – like N

• Intent – To perform inter-communication network Operation between activities or services

• Resource Externalization – such as strings and graphics

• Notification signaling users – light, sound, icon, notification, dialog etc

17. What is the Android Open Source Project?

A. We use the phrase "Android Open Source Project" or "AOSP" to refer to the people, the processes, and the source code that make up Android.

18. Why did we open the Android source code?

A . Google started the Android project in response to our own experiences launching mobile apps. We wanted to make sure that there would always be an open platform available for carriers, OEMs, and developers to use to make their innovative ideas a reality. We also wanted to make sure that there was no central point of failure, so that no single industry player could restrict or control the innovations of any other. The single most important goal of the Android Open-Source Project (AOSP) is to make sure that the open-source Android software is implemented as widely and compatibly as possible, to everyone's benefit.

31. How is Mono for Android licensed?

A. Mono for Android is a commercial/proprietary offering that is built on top of the open source Mono project and is licensed on a per-developer basis.

32. What is the API profile exposed by Mono for Android?

A. Mono for Android uses the same API profile for the core libraries as MonoTouch.Specifically, MonoTouch and Mono for Android both support a Silverlight-based API, without Silverlight's UI libraries (e.g. no XML, no WindowsBase.dll, etc.), and free of the sandboxing limitations of Silverlight.

33. Are the Android releases available in a ROM?

A. No, Android is not yet available in a ROM format.Currently Android is installed by using a clean SD Card, and booted from there.It is booted by running a special application called 'Haret.exe' residing on your SD Card which will terminate the Windows kernel and boot into Linux/Android.It can't easily be run from ROM because a) it's too experimental to risk putting in ROM and then killing a device and b) WinMo does some hardware initialization that isn't documented, but is needed before Android can run.

34. When will it be available in a ROM?

A. No time soon. Folks are working on it, but you'll need a lot of patience before it (if ever) arrives

35. How do I turn off, or reboot Android?

A. In earlier releases, you had to pull the battery or press the reset button, in newer releases, you can hold down the 'end call' button and see a menu.

36. Should we jump in to Android? What's the guarantee that's what I will see on a phone? Will service providers turn off things?

A. Keep in mind it hasn't shipped yet, this is the most interesting time. Once it is open source, it could be locked down… they could create a derivative work.

We're going to provide a piece of technology that tests the APIs. No time frame yet. The script will exercise the system. It's a compatibility test suite, to make sure nothing got disabled or broken by accident, and also ensure that apps will work across OEMs.

37. What if my app uses location API, and service provider shuts that off, can they?

A. They can do that… it's not a perfect world. Rather than having us dictate what carriers and OEMs support, we let developers develop killer apps that will require it.

We want to ensure all the application development that goes on for Android… we want to give OEMs an incentive to keep things open. It's a positive, self fulfilling vision.

38.If I'm a game developer and I'm building piece of content and I want to sell it, how do I do that and realize revenue?

A. Content distribution — we've thought of that. It'd be great if there were a place where people could go to safely download and pay for content.

39. We use SMS interception for system signalling. Is there a mechanism for an app to respond and stop the signaling chain? Is there security around that so that one vendor can't hijack a message and respond to it?

A. There's a mechanism where an application can register to receive a message with a certain signature and prevent others from getting it. We have a system of permissions apps are able to declare, enforce, and require to perform certain operations. Things like dial the phone, get to contacts, etc.. But these aren't things that are baked in the core of the system. An arbitrary app could declare custom permissions.

As far as restricting another app, the model we've been going by... the phone is not controlled by the application vendor, it's controlled by the user. Whether or not the permissions are granted is up to the user that owns the phone. If you created a protocol that intercepts an SMS and another party wrote an app that intercepts the same SMS and the user wants to use that, the user could be free to stick that in.

40. Can the user set a priority?

A. Don't know, post your question to the developer's community board.

41. In a previous release, XMPP was turned into GTalk. Will a future version have XMPP?

A. Goal is to have XMPP support after 1.0. [Later they said both GTalk and XMPP were post 1.0 features. -Ed]

42. What's so special about Android?

A. Unlike the proprietary iPhone operating system (now known as "iOS,"), which is under the complete control of Apple — and the same goes for Research in Motion's BlackBerry OS or Microsoft's Windows Phone platform — Google released Android as an open-source OS under the auspices of the Open Handset Alliance, leaving phone manufacturers (relatively) free to tweak Android as they see fit for a given handset.

That's one thing that's special about Android. Another thing is that it just happens to be a really good OS, the first one in the post-iPhone wireless era to really give Apple a run for its money. Android may not be as sleek or polished as iOS (that's my humble opinion, at least), but it's fast and powerful, with an intuitive user interface that's packed with options and flexibility. It's also being constantly improved courtesy of the big brains at Google, making the Android experience sleeker by the day.

43. Are Android phones called "Droids"?

A. Not necessarily. "Droid" is a brand name used by Verizon Wireless for its Android-based phones — the Droid X, the Droid Eris, the Droid Incredible and so on. The HTC Evo 4G on Sprint is not a "Droid," per se, but it's still an Android smartphone.

50. What are the hottest new Android phones out right now?

A. Well, earlier this summer we got the HTC Evo 4G, which supports Sprint's budding, next-generation WiMax data network and boasts a 4.3-inch display — the same size as the screen on the Motorola Droid X, another eye-popper of a phone, except it's on Verizon instead of Sprint. Samsung is in the midst of releasing a series of what it calls its Galaxy S-class Android phones: They're thin and light, they all have high-contrast 4-inch "Super AMOLED" screens, and they're available (or will be soon) on all four of the big U.S. carriers. If you're looking for an Android phone with a slide-out QWERTY, consider the new Motorola Droid 2 on Verizon or the upcoming Samsung Epic 4G for Sprint.

51. How will you record a phone call in Android? How to get a handle on Audio Stream for a call in Android?

A. Permissions.PROCESS_OUTGOING_CALLS: Allows an application to monitor, modify, or abort outgoing calls.

52. Why cannot you run standard Java bytecode on Android?

A. Android uses Dalvik Virtual Machine (DVM) which requires a special bytecode. We need to convert Java class files into Dalvik Executable files using an Android tool called "dx". In normal circumstances, developers will not be using this tool directly and build tools will care for the generation of DVM compatible files.

53. Can you deploy executable JARs on Android? Which packaging is supported by Android?

A. No. Android platform does not support JAR deployments. Applications are packed into Android Package (.apk) using Android Asset Packaging Tool (aapt) and then deployed on to Android platform. Google provides Android Development Tools for Eclipse that can be used to generate Android Package.

54. Android application can only be programmed in Java?

A. False. You can program Android apps in C/C++ using NDK .

55. What is an action?
A. The Intent Sender desires something or doing some task

56. What are Dalvik Executable files?

A. Dalvik Executable files have .dex extension and are zipped into a single .apk file on the device.

57. How does Android system track the applications?

A. Android system assigns each application a unique ID that is called Linux user ID. This ID is used to track each application.

58. When does Android start and end an application process?

A. Android starts an application process when application's component needs to be executed. It then closes the process when it's no longer needed (garbage collection).

59. How can two Android applications share same Linux user ID and share same VM?

A. The applications must sign with the same certificate in order to share same Linux user ID and share same VM.

60. Can I use the GoToMeeting app for Android on my Android device?*****

A. Yes. If you're running Android 2.2 or higher, you can install the GoToMeeting app from the Android Market to join meetings and webinars as an attendee. We recommend using devices with a 1Ghz processor or higher for optimal performance.

61. How can I download the GoToMeeting app?

A. You can download the GoToMeetng app from the Android Market by signing in to your Google account linked with your Android device and searching for the GoToMeeting app to install it. If you don't see an Install button, you may not be running Android 2.2 or higher – the minimum system requirement needed to install the GoToMeeting app.

You can also download the GoToMeeting app from the Amazon Appstore (only available in the U.S.), which lets you instantly download the GoToMeeting app to an Android device.

If you have the GoToMeeting app pre-loaded onto your device, you'll need to first upgrade to the latest version of GoToMeeting. To upgrade, select the GoToMeeting daisy icon and then select the Upgrade button to install the most recent version of the app.

62. If I have a Motorola Android-based device that doesn't have the Android Market app, can I still download the GoToMeeting app?

A. Yes. Attendees using Motorola Android-based devices in China can now download the GoToMeeting app from SHOP4APPS™ – Motorola's preinstalled Android application storefront. The GoToMeeting app is not yet localized in Chinese, but it is available in English, German, French, Spanish and Italian.

63. What made you jump into Android all of a sudden? Why not iOS or other mobile platforms?

A. Maxim Petrov: I've never intended to do any mobile startup, but I got an Android phone first (Nexus One), not iPhone, so I started to look into this platform first. The lack of Google's own music app was obvious. I think if it was iPhone, not Nexus One, I could go developing for iOS instead. Though, you know, there are a lot more really good apps that already exist for iOS (and existed a year ago), all niches are filled, Apple is pretty restrictive (I don't think PowerAMP iPhone version would have ever been accepted in the Appstore). You can jump into Android quickly - just download the SDK, install adb driver, and you can develop - for your phone, for your friends (first beta testers), it's much easier to start on Android, but I can only compare to what I've read about iOS development as I haven't developed anything for iPhone.

64. What were your initial impressions of Android development?

A.Maxim Petrov: Android developing (and actually, any software developing) is not about knowing the language - languages are just tools, so adding a tool to a toolbox is usually not a problem (I moved to Android/Java/C dev right from Ruby - and these are completely different languages). Given experience with any other languages, you can move to Android pretty quickly, at least start prototyping something, though, you need to fight the initial quirks (like SDK installation, lack of good documentation, android SDK/Eclipse and framework bugs, and the Android core devs' "you can't do that, please don't do that").Android development infrastructure is very immature, while Android end user can never notice the immaturity of the platform (as actually, it's not so immature on end user side), the development side of things is really lacking in many areas.

For example, documentation is lacking, often conflicts with real state of things and it's just not enough. Though, this is balanced by the fact that Android is open source - you can just go check the source, and the source is the best documentation, but you need to get used (I am) to this approach. For example, Honeycomb sources are not published yet, and this immediately raised questions, like how do they activate that menu button in bottom status bar.

65. Does Android support Adobe Flash in the browser?

A.Flash support varies by device with Android 2.1. The Samsung Acclaim does not have Flash support upon launch, but the HTC Desire will support Flash Lite 4.0 running Android 2.1. Flash 10.1 support is coming to Android-powered phones with Android 2.2.

66.Does Android support push email or is it pull?

 A. Android 2.1 supports push e-mail for Exchange mail and Gmail.

67. Will these phones have world phone capabilities, with the ability to make calls, receive data in other countries? Or will they be able to use Google Voice to make calls?

A.Our Android-powered phones have Wi-Fi which can be used abroad for data, including Google Voice for making international calls. International Roaming for voice is available in several countries.

68. Will the App run on my Android phone?

A. Yes, our App is fully compatible with any Android phone running Android software v2.1 or later.

69. How do I install your App?

 A. You can install our App from the Android Market by following the below steps:

Open the Android Market application in the Applications menu.

Hit the search icon and type in E.ON

To install it, hit the 'Free' button on the left hand side

In the next screen, it will give you more details about the application including the different functionalities it will need to access. Just click on OK to finish installing the application.

70. How do I find and download updates to the E.ON Android application?

A. Any updates to our App will appear on your notification menu at the top of your screen. Just tap on the E.ON App icon and you'll be taken into the Android Market and be presented with the E.ON App download page.

71. What do I do if I have problems downloading your App?

A. If you receive a "Download unsuccessful" message when trying to download our App you can try the following steps:

Restart your phone and then try downloading the app again.

Make sure that you're connected to your network – if you're not you'll need to contact your mobile service provider

Wait up to 10 minutes and try to download our App again.

If you get stuck at "Starting download" then:

Make sure that you're connected to your network – if you're not you'll need to contact your mobile service provider

If your request to download our App doesn't start at all then try the below:

Check your connectivity as stated above

Make sure that your phone has enough available space to install our App. If you need to, try uninstalling some apps that you don't use anymore or moving them to your SD card.

Request the download again using Android Market from your device.

72. What is an Intent?
A class (Intent) which describes what a caller desires to do. The caller will send this intent to Android's intent resolver, which finds the most suitable activity for the intent. E.g. opening a PDF document is an intent, and the Adobe Reader apps will be the perfect activity for that intent (class).

73. What is a Sticky Intent?

A. Sticky Intent is also a type of Intent which allows a communication between a function and a service sendStickyBroadcast() performs a sendBroadcast(Intent) known as sticky, i.e. the Intent you are sending stays around after the broadcast is complete, so that others can quickly retrieve that data through the return value of registerReceiver(BroadcastReceiver, IntentFilter). In all other ways, this behaves the same as sendBroadcast(Intent). One example of a sticky broadcast sent via the operating system is ACTION_BATTERY_CHANGED. When you call registerReceiver() for that action -- even with a null BroadcastReceiver -- you get the Intent that was last broadcast for that action. Hence, you can use this to find the state of the battery without necessarily registering for all future state changes in the battery.

74. How the nine-patch Image different from a regular bitmap? Alternatively, what is the difference between nine-patch Image vs regular Bitmap Image?

A.It is one of a resizable bitmap resource which is being used as backgrounds or other images on the device. The NinePatch class allows drawing a bitmap in nine sections. The four corners are unscaled; the middle of the image is scaled in both axes, the four edges are scaled into one axis.

75. What is a resource?

A. user defined JSON, XML, bitmap, or other file, injected into the application build process, which can later be loaded from code.

76.How will you record a phone call in Android? or How to handle an Audio Stream for a call in Android?

Permission.PROCESS_OUTGOING_CALLS: Will Allow an application to monitor, modify, or abort outgoing calls. So using that permission we can monitor the Phone calls.

77.Does Android support the Bluetooth serial port profile?
   Yes.

78. Can an application be started on powerup?
Yes.

79. How to Translate in Android?
The Google translator translates the data of one language into another language by using XMPP to transmit data. You can type the message in English and select the language which is understood by the citizens of the country in order to reach the message to the citizens.

80. Describe Briefly the Android Application Architecture
Android Application Architecture has the following components:

Services like Network Operation
Intent - To perform inter-communication between activities or servicesResource Externalization - such as strings and graphics
Notification signaling users - light, sound, icon, notification, dialog etc.

Content Providers - They share data between applications

81. What is needed to make a multiple choice list with a custom view for each row?
A. Multiple choice list can be viewed by making the CheckBox android:id value be "@android:id /text1". That is the ID used by Android for the CheckedTextView in simple_list_item_multiple_choice.

82. What dialog boxes are supported in Android ?Android supports 4 dialog boxes:

- AlertDialog: An alert dialog box supports 0 to 3 buttons and a list of selectable elements, including check boxes and radio buttons. Among the other dialog boxes, the most suggested dialog box is the alert dialog box.

- ProgressDialog: This dialog box displays a progress wheel or a progress bar. It is an extension of AlertDialog and supports adding buttons.
- DatePickerDialog: This dialog box is used for selecting a date by the user.
- TimePickerDialog: This dialog box is used for selecting time by the user.

83.Introduction Android:

Android is an operating system for mobile devices that includes middleware and key applications, and uses a modified version of the Linux kernel. It was initially developed by Android Inc..It allows developers to write managed code in the Java language, controlling the device via Google-developed Java libraries…..

The Android SDK includes a comprehensive set of development tools . These include a debugger, libraries, a handset emulator (based on QEMU), documentation, sample code, and tutorials. Currently supported development platforms include x86-architecture computers running Linux (any modern desktop Linux distribution), Mac OS X 10.4.8 or later, Windows XP or Vista.

Android does not use established Java standards, i.e. Java SE and ME. This prevents compatibility among Java applications written for those platforms and those for the Android platform. Android only reuses the Java language syntax, but does not provide the full-class libraries and APIs bundled with Java SE or ME

84.Features of Android:

Application framework enabling reuse and replacement of components

Dalvik virtual machine optimized for mobile devices

Integrated browser based on the open source WebKit engine

Optimized graphics powered by a custom 2D graphics library; 3D graphics based on the OpenGL ES 1.0 specification (hardware acceleration optional)

SQLite for structured data storage

Media support for common audio, video, and still image formats (MPEG4, H.264, MP3, AAC, AMR, JPG, PNG, GIF)

GSM Telephony (hardware dependent)

Bluetooth, EDGE, 3G, and WiFi (hardware dependent)

Camera, GPS, compass, and accelerometer (hardware dependent)

Rich development environment including a device emulator, tools for debugging, memory and performance profiling, and a plugin for the Eclipse IDE.

85.What is an Application ?

A. Collection of one or more activities, services, listeners, and intent receivers. An application has a single manifest, and is compiled into a single .apk file on the device.

86.What is a Content Provider ?

A. A class built on ContentProvider that handles content query strings of a specific format to return data in a specific format. See Reading and writing data to a content provider for information on using content providers.

87. What is a Dalvik ?

A. The name of Android's virtual machine. The Dalvik VM is an interpreter-only virtual machine that executes files in the Dalvik Executable (.dex) format, a format that is optimized for efficient storage and memory-mappable execution. The virtual machine is register-based, and it can run classes compiled by a Java language compiler that have been transformed into its native format using the included "dx" tool. The VM runs on top of Posix-compliant operating systems, which it relies on for underlying functionality (such as threading and low level memory management). The Dalvik core class library is intended to provide a familiar development base for those used to programming with Java Standard Edition, but it is geared specifically to the needs of a small mobile device.

88.What is an DDMS ?

A. Dalvik Debug Monitor Service, a GUI debugging application shipped with the SDK. It provides screen capture, log dump, and process examination capabilities.

89.What is Drawable?

A. A compiled visual resource that can be used as a background, title, or other part of the screen. It is compiled into an android.graphics.drawable subclass.

90.What are fragments in Android Activity ?

A. Fragment represents a behavior or a portion of user interface in an Activity. And it is a self-contained component with its own UI and lifecycle.

91. What is Service?

A. Service doesn't have a visual user interface , but rather runs in the background for an indefinite period of time. For Example, a service might play background for music as the user attends to other matters.

92. What is BroadReceivers?

A. BroadcastReceiver is a component that does nothing but receive and react to broadcast announcements.

For example, the battery is low or that the user changed a language preference.

93. Android latest Version?

A. Android 4.0.3

94.How many ways data stored in Android?

1.SharedPreferences

2.Internal Storage

3.External Storage

4.SQLite Database

5.Network connection

95. Types of Android applications?

1.Foreground

2.Background

3.Intermittent

4.Widget

96. Android Development Tools?

A. The Android SDK and Virtual Device Manager Used to create and manage Android Virtual Devices (AVD) and SDK packages.

The Android Emulator An implementation of the Android virtual machine designed to run within a virtual device on your development computer. Use the emulator to test and debug your Android applications.

Dalvik Debug Monitoring Service(DDMS) Use the DDMS perspective to monitor and control the Dalvik virtual machines on which your debugging your application.

Android Asset Packaging Tool(AAPT) Constructs the destributable Android packages files (.apk).

Android Debug Bridge(ADB) A client-server application that provedes a link to a running emulator.It lets you copy files, install compiled application packages(.apk),and run shell commands.

97.What is View in Android?

A. Views are the base class for all visual interface elements(commonly known as controls or widgets).

All UI controls,including the layout classes,are derived for View.

98. What View Group in Android?

A. View Groups are extensions of the View class that can contain multiple child View.Extend the ViewGroup class to create compound controls made up of interconnected child Views.

99.Implicent Intents and Late Runtime Binding?

A. An implicit Intent is mechanism that lets anonymous application components service action request.

That means you can ask the system to launch an Activity that can perform a given action without knowing which application ,or Activity , will do so.

100. What are Native Android Actions?

A. Native Android applications also use Intents to launch Activities and sub Activities

ACTION-ANSWER Opens an Activity that handles immediately initiates a call using the number supplied in the Intent URI. Genereally it's considered better from to use ACTION_DIAL if possible.

ACTION_DELETE Starts an Activity hat lets you delete the data specified at that Intent's data URI.

ACTION_DIAL Brings up a dialer application with the number to dial pre-populated from the Intent URI. By default this is handled by the native Android phone dialer.

ACTION_EDIT Requests an Activity that can edit that data at the specified Intent URI.

ACTION_INSERT

ACTION_PICK

ACTION_SEARCH

ACTION_SENDTO

ACTION_SEND

ACTION_VIEW

ACTION_WEB_SEARCH

101.What is Pending Intent?

A.The PendingIntent class provides a mechanism for creating Intents that can be fired by another application at a later time. A pending Intent is commonly used to package an Intent will be fired in response to a future event,such as a widget View being clicked or a Notification being selected from the notification panel.

102. What is Adapter?

A. Adapter are bridging classes that bind data to Views(such as List Views) used in the user interface.

The adapter is responsible for creating for creating the child Views used to represent each item within

the parent View, and providing access to the underlying data.

General Android questions

- The Activity life cycle is must. Different phases of Activity Life cycle. For example: when and how the activity comes to foreground?
- Different Kinds of Intents
- Different Kinds of Context
- Different Storage Methods in android
- Kinds of Log debugger and Debugger Configuration
- How to debug the application on real device.
- How do you ensure that the app design will be consistent across the different screen resolutions
- Thread concepts also plus points as we deal with the treads more.
- Can you able to build custom views and how?
- How to create flexible layouts, For example to place English, Chinese fonts.
- What is localization and how to achieve?
- How to avoid ANR status
- How to do Memory management
- Inter Process Communication (IPC)
- What is onCreate(Bundle savedInstanceState), Have you used savedInstanceState when and why?
- Fragments in an Activity
- When to use a service
- How to use a broadcast receiver and register it both in the manifest and in code
- Intent filters
- The types of flags to run an application
- How to do data intensive calculations using threads
- Passing large objects (that can't be passed via intents and shouldn't be serialized) via a service
- Binding to a service and the service lifecycle
- How to persist data (both savedInstanceState and more permanent ways)

What is stickey intent?

Perform a sendBroadcast(Intent) that is "sticky," meaning the Intent you are sending stays around after the broadcast is complete, so that others can quickly retrieve that data through the return value of registerReceiver(BroadcastReceiver, IntentFilter). In all other ways, this behaves the same as sendBroadcast(Intent).

One example of a sticky broadcast sent via the operating system is ACTION_BATTERY_CHANGED. When you call registerReceiver() for that action -- even with a null BroadcastReceiver -- you get the Intent that was last broadcast for that action. Hence, you can use this to find the state of the battery without necessarily registering for all future state changes in the battery.

```
Intent intent = new Intent("some.custom.action");
intent.putExtra("some_boolean", true);
sendStickyBroadcast(intent);
```

If you are listening for this broadcast in an Activity that was frozen (onPause), you could miss the actual event. This allows you to check the broadcast after it was fired (onResume).

EDIT: More on sticky boradcasts...

Also check out removeStickyBroadcast(Intent), and on API Level 5 +, isInitialStickyBroadcast() for usage in the Receiver's onReceive.

1. The Intent Class

The Intent class has acquired two rather specialized factory methods.

The method

 public static Intent makeMainActivity(ComponentName mainActivity)

will return an Intent which can be used to launch an Application with the named main Activity.

For example,

```
Intent i = Intent.makeMainActivity(
               new ComponentName(
                   "xper.honeycomb",
                   "xper.honycomb.XperActivity"));

   System.out.println("action      == " + i.getAction());
   System.out.println("categories == " + i.getCategories());
   System.out.println("component  == " + i.getComponent());
   System.out.println("flags       == 0x" + Integer.toHexString(i.getFlags()));
```

 prints

```
   action    == android.intent.action.MAIN
   categories == [android.intent.category.LAUNCHER]
   component == ComponentInfo{xper.honeycomb/xper.honycomb.XperActivity}
   flags      == 0x0
```

The method

 public static Intent makeRestartActivityTask(ComponentName mainActivity)

will return an Intent to re-launch an Application with the named main Activity.

For example,

```
   Intent j = Intent.makeRestartActivityTask(
               new ComponentName(
                   "xper.honeycomb",
                   "xper.honycomb.XperActivity"));

   System.out.println("action      == " + j.getAction());
   System.out.println("categories == " + j.getCategories());
```

```
System.out.println("component == " + j.getComponent());
System.out.println("flags     == 0x" + Integer.toHexString(j.getFlags()));
```

prints

```
action     == android.intent.action.MAIN
categories == [android.intent.category.LAUNCHER]
component  == ComponentInfo{xper.honeycomb/xper.honycomb.XperActivity}
flags      == 0x10008000
```

As can be seen the difference between the two methods is that the second one sets two flags,

Intent.FLAG_ACTIVITY_NEW_TASK(0x10000000)

and

Intent.FLAG_ACTIVITY_CLEAR_TASK(0x00008000))

Quite why it is necessary to add two brand new methods for this purpose is not that obvious.

2. Activities And Intents

The method

public abstract void startActivities(Intent[] intents)

has been added to the class android.app.Content

An implementation of this method will effectively start a stack of Activities with the Activity at the bottom corresponding to the first Intent in the array and the Activity at the top corresponding to the last Intent in the array. When started in this way an Activity is not created until it is actually accessed by the User

For example, if an Application defines the following Activities

```
<activity
   android:name  = "Foo"
   android:label = "Foo">
   <intent-filter>
     <action
       android:name = "xper.intent.FOO_INTENT"/>
     <category
       android:name = "android.intent.category.DEFAULT"/>
   </intent-filter>
</activity>
<activity
   android:name  = "Bar"
   android:label = "Bar">
```

```
      <intent-filter>
        <action
          android:name = "xper.intent.BAR_INTENT"/>
        <category
          android:name = "android.intent.category.DEFAULT"/>
      </intent-filter>
    </activity>
    <activity
      android:name  = "Baz"
      android:label = "Baz">
      <intent-filter>
        <action
          android:name = "xper.intent.BAZ_INTENT"/>
        <category
          android:name = "android.intent.category.DEFAULT"/>
      </intent-filter>
    </activity>
```

and it executes

```
    startActivities(
      new Intent[]
      {
        new Intent("xper.intent.FOO_INTENT"),
        new Intent("xper.intent.BAR_INTENT"),
        new Intent("xper.intent.BAZ_INTENT")
      });
```

then an instance of Baz is created and made the current Activity.

If Baz finishes then an instance of Bar is created and is made the current Activity.

If Bar finishes then an instance of Foo is created and is made the current Activity.

The method documentation states

This method throws ActivityNotFoundException if there was no Activity found for any given Intent. In this case state of the activity stack is undefined (some Intents in the list may be on it, some not), so you probably want to avoid such situations.

which is not that helpful.

What currently appears to happen in practice is that as long as the ActivityNotFoundException is caught all the Activities corresponding to the Intents before the one that cannot be resolved are started.

There is no mention of whether this method *plays nicely* with things like the Intent.FLAG_ACTIVITY_CLEAR_TOP flag and other of that ilk should you be sufficiently adventurous to set them in any of the given Intents.

3. Broadcast Intents

The BroadcastReceiver class has acquired an inner class

   PendingResult

and a new method

   public final PendingResult goAsync()

This method makes it possible for a BroadcastReceiver to complete the handling of a broadcast Intent after its onReceive() method has returned. This is done by handing off the returned PendingResult instance to a different thread which can then do the necessary work before using the PendingResult instance to complete the broadcast.

The PendingResult class defines almost the same set of methods for manipulating the broadcast Intent as the BroadcastReceiver class plus the additional method

   public final void finish()

which is used to indicate that the handling of the broadcast Intent has been completed.

The only documentation on this feature appears to be the finish() method documentation, and the PendingResult class
documentation.

The BroadcastReceiver class documentation is otherwise unchanged.

For example

A BroadcastReceiver object is only valid for the duration of the call to onReceive(Context, Intent). Once your code returns from this function, the system considers the object to be finished and no longer active.

which is no longer necessarily true, which is a bit unfortunate.

In the absence of any additional documentation some experiments reveal the following

- The finish() method works for both dynamically and statically registered BroadcastReceivers.
- The finish() method works for
  - normal
  - ordered, and
  - sticky

   broadcast Intents.

- The process running a dynamically registered BroadcastReceiver will be killed if the finish() method is not called within approximately ten seconds of the call to the goAsync() method if it is an ordered broadcast, but not otherwise.

- The process running a statically registered BroadcastReceiver will be killed if the finish() method is not called within approximately ten seconds of the call to the goAsync() method irrespective of the type of the broadcast.

Given the upper limit on the amount of time which can elapse whilest a broadcast Intent is being handled asynchronously it is not clear how useful this feature actually. Presumably somebody out there needs it for something. Either that or somebody added it for a bet.

4. IntentSenders And PendingIntents

The PendingIntent class has acquired a fourth factory method

    public static PendingIntent getActivities(Context context, int requestCode, Intent[] intents, int flags)

Invoking the resulting IntentSender/PendingIntent is equivalent to calling an implementation of the
Context.startActivities()
method.

The documentation for this method is a bit confusing. On the one hand it states (emphasis added)

The **first** Intent in the array is taken as the primary key for the PendingIntent, like the single Intent given to getActivity(Context, int, Intent, int).

and on the other (emphasis added again)

The *last* intent in the array represents the key for the PendingIntent. In other words, it is the significant element for matching (as done with the single intent given to getActivity(Context, int, Intent, int), its content will be the subject of replacement by send(Context, int, Intent) and FLAG_UPDATE_CURRENT, etc. This is because it is the most specific of the supplied intents, and the UI the user actually sees when the intents are started.

On the basis of some experiments (currently the source code for this is not available) it is the second version which is correct.

---

1. The Broadcast Intent Model

- Any Application can send a broadcast Intent.
- To receive broadcast Intents an Application must register a BroadcastReceiver.
- An Application can register multiple BroadcastReceivers.
- An Application can register BroadcastReceivers statically and/or dynamically.
- A BroadcastReceiver can be registered with an associated Intent Filter.
- The Intent Filter is used to specify which broadcast Intents the BroadcastReceiver wishes to receive.

- A *normal* broadcast Intent is sent *asynchronously* and the ordering of its delivery to the set of BroadcastReceivers eligible to receive it is undefined.
- An *ordered* broadcast Intent is delivered sequentially to each member of the set of BroadcastReceivers eligible to receive it in the order defined by the priority of the associated IntentFilters.
- An ordered broadcast Intent can have additional data associated with it in the form of
  - a code (an int),
  - data (a String), and
  - extras (a Bundle)
- The initial values of the additional data can be specified by the sender of the ordered broadcast Intent
- The current values of the additional data can be read and/or replaced by each BroadcastReceiver which receives the ordered broadcast Intent
- Any BroadcastReceiver which receives an ordered broadcast Intent can stop the sending process
- The sender of an ordered broadcast Intent can specify that it be *notified* when the broadcast has *completed*
- The sender of an ordered broadcast Intent can access the final values of the additional data when it is notified that the broadcast has completed.
- A broadcast Intent can be specified to be *sticky* in which case it will be retained by the system after it has been sent.
- A sticky broadcast Intent can be removed after it has been sent.
- BroadcastReceivers dynamically registered after a sticky broadcast Intent has been sent, and not subsequently removed, will still receive it if all other the criteria for receiving it have been met.
- A sticky broadcast Intent can be retrieved at any time after it has been sent without registering a BroadcastReceiver.
- An Application can specify a permission when sending a normal or ordered broadcast Intent.
- A BroadcastReceiver cannot receive a normal or ordered broadcast Intent sent with an associated permission if the Application that registered the BroadcastReceiver has not been granted that permission.
- An Application can specify a permission when registering a BroadcastReceiver.
- A BroadcastReceiver registered with an associated permission cannot receive any normal or ordered broadcast Intent sent by an Application which has not been granted that permission.

When used in this way Intents are effectively *Events* and BroadcastReceivers are *Event Handlers/Listeners*.

2. The BroadcastReceiver Class

The class android.content.BroadcastReceiver is abstract. To receive broadcast Intents a sub-class must be defined which implements the method

public abstract void onReceive(Context context, Intent intent)

It is this method which is invoked when a broadcast Intent satisfies the criteria the BroadcastReceiver was registered with.

3. Registering Broadcast Receivers Statically

An Application can declare Broadcast Receivers in its manifest (the AndroidManifest.xml file), by defining one or more receiver elements, as children of the application element.

3.1 The receiver Element

3.1.1 Attributes

3.1.1.1 The enabled Attribute

The enabled attribute is optional. If present its value can be either "true" or "false"

If the value is "true" then the System can create instances of the BroadcastReceiver and it can function normally.

If the value is "false" then the System cannot create instances of the BroadcastReceiver and it is not functional.

The default value is "true".

If the Application itself is not enabled then the BroadcastReceiver is not functional.

3.1.1.2 The exported Attribute

The exported attribute is optional. If present its value can be either "true" or "false".

If the value is "true" then the BroadcastReceiver can, if all other criteria are met, receive broadcast Intents from any Application.

If the value is "false" then the BroadcastReceiver can only receive broadcast Intents from the registering Application or other Applications with the same User Id even if the other specified criteria are met.

The default value is "true" if the registered BroadcastReceiver has one or more IntentFilters associated with it. Otherwise it is "false".

3.1.1.3 The icon Attribute

The icon attribute is optional. If present it should specify a Drawable resource. This will be used by the System to visually identify the BroadcastReceiver to the User if necessary.

3.1.1.4 The label Attribute

The label attribute is optional. If present it should specify a String resource. This will be used by the System to identify the BroadcastReceiver to the User if necessary.

3.1.1.5 The name Attribute

The name attribute is mandatory. It specifies the name of the BroadcastReceiver class.

The documentation for this attribute states

This should be a fully qualified class name (such as, "com.example.project.ReportReceiver"). However, as a shorthand, if the first character of the name is a period (for example, ". ReportReceiver"), it is appended to the package name specified in the <manifest> element.

Which is true as far as it goes.

By default the Android ADT Eclipse plugin actually generates receiver elements that look like this

```
<receiver android:name="XperBroadcastReceiver"></receiver>
```

The attribute value is simply the unqualified class name and this also works.

3.1.1.6 The permission Attribute

The permission attribute is optional. If present then the BroadcastReceiver cannot receive broadcast Intents sent by Applications which have not been granted the specified permission.

3.1.1.7 The process Attribute

The process attribute is optional. If present it specifies the process in which the Systen should create the BroadcastReceiver when necessary.

3.1.2 Child Elements

The receiver element can have two child elements

intent-filter

and

meta-data

Both elements are optional. If present both elements can occur multiple times.

4. Registering And Unregistering BroadcastReceivers Dynamically

4.1 Registration

A BroadcastReceiver can be registered dynamically using an implementation of the android.content.Context

```
public abstract Intent registerReceiver(
                BroadcastReceiver receiver,
                IntentFilter    filter,
                String          broadcastPermission,
                Handler         scheduler)
```

method.

If the broadcastPermission argument is non-null then the registered BroadcastReceiver cannot receive broadcast Intents from any Application which has not been granted the specified permission.

If the scheduler argument is non-null then the registered BroadcastReceiver's onReceive() method will be executed in the context of the specified Handler.

If it is not necessary to specify either a permission or a Handler then an implementation of the android.content.Context

```
public abstract Intent registerReceiver(
                BroadcastReceiver receiver,
                IntentFilter    filter)
```

method can be used instead.

Both methods will return either a broadcast Intent which was sent in sticky mode which matches the given IntentFilter, or null. (See also).

Both methods can also be used to access a stick broadcast Intent directly.

The same BroadcastReceiver can be registered multiple times with different IntentFilters.

4.2 Unregistration

A dynamically registered BroadcastReceiver can be unregistered using an implementation of the android.content.Context

```
public abstract void unregisterReceiver(BroadcastReceiver receiver)
```

The effect of this method is undo the effects of all calls to either of the registerReceiver() methods used to register the given BroadcastReceiver.

5. BroadcastReceiver Lifecycles

The lifecycle of a BroadcastReceiver differs depending upon whether it was registered statically or dynamically.

5.1 The Static BroadcastReceiver Lifecycle

The lifecycle of a statically registered BroadcastReceiver is under the control of the System.

When a broadcast Intent is to be delivered to a statically registered BroadcastReceiver the System will

1. create the appropriate process in which to run it if necessary
2. create an instance of the BroadcastReceiver and invoke its onReceive() method

Once the onReceive() method has returned the System may stop the process used to run it.

The transient nature of a statically registered BroadcastReceiver means that its onReceive() method cannot use any functionality which is asynchronous, for example, binding to a Service.

This constraint is enforced by the implementation of the Context passed to the method at runtime. For example, its implementation of the bindService() method throws a RuntimeException.

5.2 The Dynamic BroadcastReceiver Lifecycle

The lifecycle of a dyamically registered BroadcastReceiver is under the control of the Application.

An Application can create BroadcastReceivers and register and unregister them as and when it chooses.

There are no constraints on the functionality that can be used by the implementation of the onReceive() method of a dynamically registered BroadcastReceiver.

6. BroadcastReceivers And Intent Resolution

If an Intent explicitly specifies a component then the Intent resolves to that Component if it is a BroadcastReceiver. If the specified Component is not a BroadcastReceiver it is equivalent to the case where the Intent cannot be resolved to any BroadcastReceiver(s).

Otherwise a search is made for all BroadcastReceivers with an associated IntentFilter which matches the given Intent, as defined by the IntentFilter.match() method.

If the Intent specifies a package then the search is confined to the Services in that Application package.

An Application can determine the BroadcastReceivers to which a given Intent resolves by using an implementation od the android.content.pm.PackageManager

    public abstract List queryBroadcastReceivers (Intent intent, int flags)

The list is sorted in order from high to low priority as defined by the associated IntentFilters.

7. Broadcasting

A normal broadcast Intent can be sent using an implementation of the android.content.Context

    public abstract void sendBroadcast(Intent intent, String receiverPermission)

method.

If the receiverPermission argument is non-null then a BroadcastReceiver cannot receive the broadcast Intent being sent unless it was declared by an Application which has been granted the given permission.

The method is asynchronous. It returns immediately, and the delivery of the broadcast Intent to the set of eligible BroadcastReceivers executes independently of the method's caller.

If it is not necessary to specify a permission then an implementation of the android.content.Context

```
public abstract void sendBroadcast(Intent intent)
```

can be used instead.

8. Ordered Broadcasting

8.1 Sending An Ordered Broadcast Intent

A simple ordered broadcast Intent can be sent using an implementation of the android.content.Context

```
public abstract void sendOrderedBroadcast(
                Intent intent,
                String receiverPermission)
```

method.

If the receiverPermission argument is non-null then a BroadcastReceiver cannot receive the broadcast Intent being sent unless it was declared by an Application which has been granted the given permission.

The method is asynchronous. It returns immediately, and the process of sending the ordered broadcast Intent executes independently of the method's caller.

8.2 Sending An Ordered Broadcast Intent And Getting A "Result"

An implementation of the android.content.Context method

```
public abstract void sendOrderedBroadcast(
                Intent              intent,
                String              receiverPermission,
                BroadcastReceiver resultReceiver,
                Handler             scheduler,
                int                 initialCode,
                String              initialData,
                Bundle              initialExtras)
```

can be used to send an ordered broadcast Intent with associated data and obtain a *result*.

If the receiverPermission argument is non-null then the broadcast Intent being sent cannot be received by any BroadcastReceiver registered by an Application which has not been granted the specified permission.

If the resultReceiver argument is non-null it specifies a BroadcastReceiver whose onReceive() method will be invoked when the sending of the ordered broadcast Intent completes.

If the scheduler argument is non-null and the resultReceiver argument is also non-null then the onReceive() method of the BroadcastReceiver will be run in the context of the specified Handler.

The

- initialCode
- initialData
- initialExtras

arguments specify the initial values of the

- code
- data
- extras

elements respectively of the additional data associated with the sending of the ordered broadcast Intent.

The method is asynchronous. It returns immediately, and the process of sending the ordered broadcast Intent executes independently of the method's caller.

8.2.1 BroadcastReceivers And Ordered Broadcast Intents

The BroadcastReceiver class defines a number of methods related to ordered broadcast Intents which can be used by an implementation of the onReceive() method.

8.2.1.1 Determining The "Type" Of A Broadcast Intent

The

```
public final boolean isOrderedBroadcast()
```

method will return true if the onReceive()method has been invoked with an ordered broadcast Intent.

8.2.1.2 Getting The Ordered Broadcast Intent "Result" Data

The methods

- public final int getResultCode()
- public final String getResultData()
- public final Bundle getResultExtras(boolean makeMap)</p

will return the current values of the

- code
- data
- extras

respectively.

If the code is not defined then the default value is -1.

If the data is not defined then the default value is null.

If the extras are not defined then the default value is null unless the makeMap argument is true in which case an empty Bundle is created and returned.

These methods can be called when the onReceive() method was not invoked on an ordered broadcast Intent and they will return the default values as above.

8.2.1.3 Setting The Ordered Broadcast Intent "Result" Data

The methods

- public final void setResultCode(int code)
- public final void setResultData(String data)
- public final void setResultExtras (Bundle extras)

will set the current values of the

- code
- data
- extras

respectively.

Alternatively all three can be set simultaneously using the

    public final void setResult(int code, String data, Bundle extras)

method.

Using any of these methods when the onReceive() method has not been invoked on an ordered broadcast Intent will result in a RuntimeException, except in one situation.

8.2.1.4 Stopping The Process Of Sending Of An Ordered Broadcast Intent

A BroadcastReceiver can stop the process of sending an ordered broadcast Intent by calling the

    public final void abortBroadcast()

method.

Any BroadcastReceivers of the same priority that have not already received the Intent and all those with a lower priority than the current BroacastReceiver will not receive the Intent.

Using this method when the onReceive() method has not been invoked on an ordered broadcast Intent will result in a RuntimeException, except in one situation.

8.3 Ordered Broadcast Intent Examples

There are four BroadcastReceivers registered statically as follows

```
<receiver
  android:name = "OrderedBroadcastReceiverOne">
  <intent-filter
    android:priority = "1">
    <action
      android:name = "xper.example.ORDERED_BROADCAST_INTENT"/>
    <action
      android:name = "xper.example.ORDERED_BROADCAST_INTENT_ONE"/>
    <action
      android:name = "xper.example.ORDERED_BROADCAST_INTENT_TWO"/>
  </intent-filter>
</receiver>

<receiver
  android:name = "OrderedBroadcastReceiverTwoA">
  <intent-filter
    android:priority = "2">
    <action
      android:name = "xper.example.ORDERED_BROADCAST_INTENT"/>
    <action
      android:name = "xper.example.ORDERED_BROADCAST_INTENT_ONE"/>
    <action
      android:name = "xper.example.ORDERED_BROADCAST_INTENT_TWO"/>
  </intent-filter>
</receiver>

<receiver
  android:name = "OrderedBroadcastReceiverTwoB">
  <intent-filter
    android:priority = "2">
    <action
      android:name = "xper.example.ORDERED_BROADCAST_INTENT"/>
    <action
      android:name = "xper.example.ORDERED_BROADCAST_INTENT_ONE"/>
    <action
      android:name = "xper.example.ORDERED_BROADCAST_INTENT_TWO"/>
  </intent-filter>
</receiver>

<receiver
  android:name = "OrderedBroadcastReceiverThree">
  <intent-filter
    android:priority = "3">
    <action
      android:name = "xper.example.ORDERED_BROADCAST_INTENT"/>
    <action
      android:name = "xper.example.ORDERED_BROADCAST_INTENT_ONE"/>
    <action
```

```
          android:name = "xper.example.ORDERED_BROADCAST_INTENT_TWO"/>
      </intent-filter>
  </receiver>
```

Their respective onReceive() methods are defined as follows

```java
// OrderedBroadcastReceiverOne.onReceive()

public void onReceive(Context context, Intent intent)
{
    System.out.println("One: " + intent);
    System.out.println("\tgetResultCode() => " + getResultCode());
    System.out.println("\tgetResultData() => " + getResultData());
    setResultCode(getResultCode() + 1);
    setResultData(getResultData() + ", One");

    Bundle extras = getResultExtras(true);

    extras.putString("One.value", "One");
    setResultExtras(extras);
    System.out.println("One Done");
}

...

// OrderedBroadcastReceiverTwoA.onReceive()

public void onReceive(Context context, Intent intent)
{
    System.out.println("TwoA");
    System.out.println(intent);
    System.out.println("\tgetResultCode() => " + getResultCode());
    System.out.println("\tgetResultData() => " + getResultData());
    setResultCode(getResultCode() + 20);
    setResultData(getResultData() + ", TwoA");

    Bundle extras = getResultExtras(true);

    extras.putString("TwoA.value", "TwoA");
    setResultExtras(extras);
    if ("xper.example.ORDERED_BROADCAST_INTENT_TWO".equals(intent.getAction()))
    {
        abortBroadcast();
    }
    System.out.println("TwoA done");
}

...
```

```
// OrderedBroadcastReceiverTwoB.onReceive()

public void onReceive(Context context, Intent intent)
{
    System.out.println("TwoB");
    System.out.println(intent);
    System.out.println("\tgetResultCode() => " + getResultCode());
    System.out.println("\tgetResultData() => " + getResultData());
    setResultCode(getResultCode() + 20);
    setResultData(getResultData() + ", TwoB");

    Bundle extras = getResultExtras(true);

    extras.putString("TwoB.value", "TwoB");
    setResultExtras(extras);
    if ("xper.example.ORDERED_BROADCAST_INTENT_TWO".equals(intent.getAction()))
    {
        abortBroadcast();
    }
    System.out.println("TwoB done");
}

...

// OrderedBroadcastReceiverThree.onReceive()

public void onReceive(Context context, Intent intent)
{
    System.out.println("Three");
    System.out.println(intent);
    System.out.println("\tgetResultCode() => " + getResultCode());
    System.out.println("\tgetResultData() => " + getResultData());
    setResultCode(getResultCode() + 300);
    setResultData(getResultData() + ", Three");

    Bundle extras = getResultExtras(true);

    extras.putString("Three.value", "Three");
    setResultExtras(extras);
    System.out.println("Three done");
}
```

There is a class ResultReceiver which is a sub-class of the class BroadcastReceiver.
Its onReceive() method is defined as follows.

```
public void onReceive(Context context, Intent intent)
{
```

```
System.out.println("ResultReceiver");
System.out.println(intent);
System.out.println("\tgetResultCode() => " + getResultCode());
System.out.println("\tgetResultData() => " + getResultData());

Bundle extras = getResultExtras(true);

System.out.println("\tBegin Extras");
for (String key : extras.keySet())
{
    System.out.print("\t\t");
    System.out.print(key);
    System.out.print("\t=> ");
    System.out.println(extras.get(key));
}
System.out.println("\tEnd Extras");
System.out.println("ResultReceiver done");
}
```

8.3.1 Example One

Sending an ordered broadcast Intent which is handled by all the registered BroadcastReceivers.

This example illustrates the delivery of the broadcast Intent to the BroadcastReceivers in priority order, and the use of result data

8.3.1.1 Stage One: Sending The Intent

The Intent is sent as follows

```
sendOrderedBroadcast(
    new Intent(
        "xper.example.ORDERED_BROADCAST_INTENT"),
    null,
    new ResultReceiver(),
    null,
    0,
    "ExampleOne",
    null);
```

8.3.1.2 Stage Two: The Broadcast Intent Is Received By OrderedBroadcastReceiverThree

The OrderedBroadcastReceiverThree.onReceive() method prints

```
Three
Intent { act=xper.example.ORDERED_BROADCAST_INTENT
cmp=xper.example.three/.OrderedBroadcastReceiverThree }
    getResultCode() => 0
```

```
    getResultData() => ExampleOne
Three done
```

8.3.1.3 Stage Three: The Broadcast Intent Is Received By OrderedBroadcastReceiverTwoA

The OrderedBroadcastReceiverTwoA.onReceive() method prints

```
   TwoA
   Intent { act=xper.example.ORDERED_BROADCAST_INTENT
cmp=xper.example.two.a/.OrderedBroadcastReceiverTwoA }
       getResultCode() => 300
       getResultData() => ExampleOne, Three
   TwoA done
```

8.3.1.4 Stage Four: The Broadcast Intent Is Received By OrderedBroadcastReceiverTwoB

The OrderedBroadcastReceiverTwoB.onReceive() method prints

```
   TwoB
   Intent { act=xper.example.ORDERED_BROADCAST_INTENT
cmp=xper.example.two.b/.OrderedBroadcastReceiverTwoB }
       getResultCode() => 320
       getResultData() => ExampleOne, Three, TwoA
   TwoB done
```

8.3.1.5 Stage Five: The Broadcast Intent Is Received By OrderedBroadcastReceiverOne

The OrderedBroadcastReceiverOne.onReceive() method prints

```
   One: Intent { act=xper.example.ORDERED_BROADCAST_INTENT
cmp=xper.example.one/.OrderedBroadcastReceiverOne }
       getResultCode() => 340
       getResultData() => ExampleOne, Three, TwoA, TwoB
   One Done
```

8.3.1.6 Stage Six: ResultReceiver onReceive() Method Called

The ResultReceiver.onReceive() method prints

```
   ResultReceiver
   Intent { act=xper.example.ORDERED_BROADCAST_INTENT }
       getResultCode() => 341
       getResultData() => ExampleOne, Three, TwoA, TwoB, One
       Begin Extras
          Three.value        => Three
          TwoB.value         => TwoB
          TwoA.value         => TwoA
          One.value  => One
```

End Extras
ResultReceiver done

8.3.2 Example Two

Sending an ordered broadcast Intent which is handled by all the registered BroadcastRecivers but one of them stops the sending process.

8.3.2.1 Stage One: Sending The Intent

The Intent is sent as follows

```
sendOrderedBroadcast(
  new Intent(
    "xper.example.ORDERED_BROADCAST_INTENT_TWO"),
  null,
  new ResultReceiver(),
  null,
  0,
  "ExampleTwo",
  null);
```

8.3.2.2 Stage Two: The Broadcast Intent Is Received By OrderedBroadcastReceiverThree

The OrderedBroadcastReceiverThree.onReceive() method prints

```
Three
Intent { act=xper.example.ORDERED_BROADCAST_INTENT_TWO
cmp=xper.example.three/.OrderedBroadcastReceiverThree }
    getResultCode() => 0
    getResultData() => ExampleTwo
Three done
```

8.3.2.3 Stage Three: The Broadcast Intent Is Received By OrderedBroadcastReceiverTwoA

The OrderedBroadcastReceiverTwoA.onReceive() method prints

```
TwoA
Intent { act=xper.example.ORDERED_BROADCAST_INTENT_TWO
cmp=xper.example.two.a/.OrderedBroadcastReceiverTwoA }
    getResultCode() => 300
    getResultData() => ExampleTwo, Three
TwoA done
```

and stops the sending of the broadcast Intent.

8.3.2.4 Stage Four: ResultReceiver onReceive() Method Called

The ResultReceiver.onReceive() method prints

```
ResultReceiver
Intent { act=xper.example.ORDERED_BROADCAST_INTENT_TWO }
   getResultCode() => 320
   getResultData() => ExampleTwo, Three, TwoA
   Begin Extras
      Three.value        => Three
      TwoA.value         => TwoA
   End Extras
ResultReceiver done
```

8.3.3 Example Three

Sending an ordered broadcast Intent which is not handled by any of the registered BroadcastReecivers.

8.3.3.1 Stage One: Sending The Intent

The Intent is sent as follows

```
sendOrderedBroadcast(
   new Intent(
      "xper.example.ORDERED_BROADCAST_INTENT_FOUR"),
         null,
         new ResultReceiver(),
         null,
         -3,
         "ExampleThree",
         null);
```

8.3.3.2 Stage Two: ResultReceiver onReceive() Method Called

The ResultReceiver.onReceive() method prints

```
ResultReceiver
Intent { act=xper.example.ORDERED_BROADCAST_INTENT_FOUR }
   getResultCode() => -3
   getResultData() => ExampleThree
   Begin Extras
   End Extras
ResultReceiver done
```

9. Sticky Broadcast Intents

Both normal and ordered broadcasts can also be performed in sticky mode.

To send a broadcast Intent in sticky mode an Application must have been granted the BROADCAST_STICKY permission.

9.1 Sending A Sticky Broadcast Intent

A normal broadcast Intent can be sent in sticky mode using an implementation of the android.content.Context

```
public abstract void sendStickyBroadcast(Intent intent)
```

method.

This works in the same way as the short-form method for sending a normal broadcast Intent.

9.2 Sending A Sticky Ordered Broadcast Intent

An ordered broadcast Intent can be sent in sticky mode using an implementation of the android.content.Context

```
public abstract void sendStickyOrderedBroadcast(
                Intent          intent,
                BroadcastReceiver resultReceiver,
                Handler          scheduler,
                int            initialCode,
                String          initialData,
                Bundle          initialExtras)
```

method.

This works in the same way as the long-form method for sending an ordered broadcast Intent.

9.3 Sticky Broadcast Intent "Replacement"

If when a broadcast Intent is sent in sticky mode it is found to *match* a sticky broadcast Intent sent previously then it will *replace*
the existing one. The Intent.filterEquals() method is used to determine whether Intents match.

One implication of this is that there can be multiple sticky broadcast Intents with, for example, the same action
but different
data URIs, since these will not match.

Conversely, broadcast Intents that differ only in their extras will match.

Note also that an ordered broadcast Intent sent in sticky mode can replace a normal broadcast Intent sent in sticky mode, and vice-versa.

For example, the following

```
IntentFilter f = new IntentFilter("xper.sticky.BROADCAST_INTENT");

sendStickyBroadcast(
  new Intent(
```

```
        "xper.sticky.BROADCAST_INTENT").
      putExtra(
        "Type",
        "Normal"));
System.out.println(registerReceiver(null, f).getStringExtra("Type"));
sendStickyOrderedBroadcast(
    new Intent(
        "xper.sticky.BROADCAST_INTENT").
      putExtra(
        "Type",
        "Ordered"),
    null,
    null,
    0,
    null,
    null);
System.out.println(registerReceiver(null, f).getStringExtra("Type"));
sendStickyBroadcast(
    new Intent(
        "xper.sticky.BROADCAST_INTENT").
      putExtra(
        "Type",
        "Normal"));
System.out.println(registerReceiver(null, f).getStringExtra("Type"));
```

will print

```
Normal
Ordered
Normal
```

9.4 Accessing A Sticky Broadcast Intent Directly

Both registerReceiver() methods can be passed a receiver argument of null. As in the non-null receiver argument case if one or more sticky broadcast Intents match the supplied IntentFilter then one of them will be returned from the method.

For example, although it is not documented as such the broadcast Intent with the action

```
android.net.conn.CONNECTIVITY_CHANGE
```

is sent in sticky mode and hence is accesible in this way.

On the emulator the following code

```
IntentFilter f = new IntentFilter(ConnectivityManager.CONNECTIVITY_ACTION);
```

```
Intent    i = registerReceiver(null, f);

System.out.println(i);

Bundle b = i.getExtras();

for (String key : b.keySet())
{
   System.out.print(key);
   System.out.print(" => ");
   System.out.println(b.get(key));
}
```

prints

```
Intent { act=android.net.conn.CONNECTIVITY_CHANGE flg=0x10000000 (has extras) }
networkInfo => NetworkInfo: type: mobile[UMTS], state: CONNECTED/CONNECTED, reason:
simLoaded, ... [elided]
  reason => simLoaded
  extraInfo => internet
  inetCondition => 0
```

Although it is possible to use the long-form of the registerReceiver() method in this way there is effectively no point since the permission argument has no effect.

For example, replacing the line

```
Intent i = registerReceiver(null, f);
```

in the example above with

```
Intent i = registerReceiver(null, f, "xper.permission.NO_SUCH_PERMISSION", null);
```

does not change the behaviour at all.

9.5 Removing A Sticky Broadcast Intent

A sticky broadcast Intent can be removed by calling an implementation of the android.content.Context method

```
public abstract void removeStickyBroadcast(Intent intent)
```

To remove a sticky broadcast Intent an Application must have been granted the BROADCAST_STICKY permission.

The method will remove the sticky broadcast Intent, if any, which *matches*, as determined by the Intent.filterEquals() method, the Intent passed as the intent argument.

9.6 Sticky Broadcast Intents And Dynamically Registered BroadcastReceivers

9.6.1 Registration

When a BroadcastReceiver is registered dynamically using the short-form registerReceiver() method, then, if the associated IntentFilter matches one or more sticky broadcast Intents

- one of the matching Intents will be returned by the method, and then, at some point
- the BroadcastReceiver's onReceive() method will be invoked for each matching sticky broadcast Intent

For example, if we define the class StickyBroadcastReceiver as follows

```
public class StickyBroadcastReceiver
        extends
            BroadcastReceiver
{
    @Override
    public void onReceive(Context context, Intent intent)
    {
        System.out.println("StickyBroadcastReceiver.onReceive(...)");
        System.out.println(intent);
        System.out.println("\tisInitialStickyBroadcast() => " + isInitialStickyBroadcast());
        System.out.println("StickyBroadcastReceiver.onReceive(...) done");
    }
}
```

then the following code

```
Intent i = registerReceiver(
        new StickyBroadcastReceiver(),
        new IntentFilter(
        ConnectivityManager.CONNECTIVITY_ACTION));

System.out.println("registerReceiver() => " + i);
```

prints

registerReceiver() => Intent { act=android.net.conn.CONNECTIVITY_CHANGE flg=0x10000000 (has extras) }

and then the onReceive() method prints

```
StickyBroadcastReceiver.onReceive(...)
Intent { act=android.net.conn.CONNECTIVITY_CHANGE flg=0x10000000 (has extras) }
    isInitialStickyBroadcast() => true
StickyBroadcastReceiver.onReceive(...) done
```

When a BroadcastReceiver is registered dynamically using the long-form registerReceiver() method then, if the associated IntentFilter matches one or more sticky broadcast Intents, the exact behaviour depends on whether or not a permission is specified.

The method will return one of the matching Intents irrespective of whether or not a permission was specified.

However, once the method has returned, if a permission was specified, then the BroadcastReceiver's onReceive() method will not be invoked on any sticky broadcast Intent sent by an Application which has not been granted that permission.

For example, modifying the previous example, then the following code

```
Intent i = registerReceiver(
        new StickyBroadcastReceiver(),
        new IntentFilter(
            ConnectivityManager.CONNECTIVITY_ACTION),
        "xper.permission.NO_SUCH_PERMISSION",
        null);
```

prints

    registerReceiver() => Intent { act=android.net.conn.CONNECTIVITY_CHANGE flg=0x10000000 (has extras) }

and that is it. The onReceive() method is not invoked.

The behaviour with respect to the onReceive() method is consistent with the way permissions work, it is really the behaviour of the registerReceiver() method which is anomalous.

9.6.2 The onReceive() Method

A dynamically registered BroadcastReceiver can determine whether it is being invoked on a sticky broadcast Intent by calling the

    public final boolean isInitialStickyBroadcast()

method.

If it is then the behaviour of some of the methods defined by the BroadcastReceiver class for use with ordered broadcast Intents is slightly different.

- The isOrderedBroadcast() method always returns false
- The methods for setting result data do not throw RuntimeExceptions, they are simply no-ops
- The abortBroadcast() method does not throw a RuntimeException, it is simply a no-op

10. Broadcast Intents And Intent Flags

There are two Intent class constants which define flags specifically for use with broadcast Intents.

10.1 FLAG_RECEIVER_REGISTERED_ONLY

If this flag is set in a broadcast Intent then it will only be delivered to those eligible BroadcastReceivers which were dynamically registered.

10.2 FLAG_RECEIVER_REPLACE_PENDING

If this flag is set in a broadcast Intent then it will replace any broadcast Intent which matches it, as defined by Intent.filterEquals(), which is currently in the process of being delivered to any eligible BroadcastReceivers.

This effect is not atomic. Some BroadcastReceivers may receive both the original and the replacement broadcast Intent, others only the replacement, as the following rather contrived example demonstrates.

We define two static BroadcastReceivers

```
<receiver
    android:name="Sole">
    <intent-filter>
      <action
        android:name="xper.receiver.intent.RECEIVER_SOLE_INTENT"/>
      <action
        android:name="xper.receiver.intent.RECEIVER_SEA_AREA_INTENT"/>
    </intent-filter>
</receiver>

<receiver
    android:name="Fastnet">
    <intent-filter>
      <action
        android:name="xper.receiver.intent.RECEIVER_FASTNET_INTENT"/>
      <action
        android:name="xper.receiver.intent.RECEIVER_SEA_AREA_INTENT"/>
    </intent-filter>
</receiver>
```

each in a separate Application, and one dynamic BroadcastReceiver registered by a third Application as follows

```
IntentFilter f = new IntentFilter();

f.addAction("xper.receiver.intent.RECEIVER_LUNDY_INTENT");
f.addAction("xper.receiver.intent.RECEIVER_SEA_AREA_INTENT");
registerReceiver(new Lundy(), f);
```

We define their respective onReceive() methods to be

```
// Sole

public void onReceive(Context context, Intent intent)
{
    System.out.println("Sole.onReceive(..., " + intent + ")");
```

```java
        System.out.println("Sole.onReceive(...) N == " + intent.getStringExtra("N"));
    }

    ...

    // Fastnet

    public void onReceive(Context context, Intent intent)
    {
        System.out.println("Fastnet.onReceive(..., " + intent + ")");
        System.out.println("Fastnet.onReceive(...) N == " + intent.getStringExtra("N"));
    }

    ...

    // Lundy

    public void onReceive(Context context, Intent intent)
    {
        System.out.println("Lundy.onReceive(..., " + intent + ")");
        System.out.println("Lundy.onReceive(...) N == " + intent.getStringExtra("N"));
    }
```

If we execute the following

```java
    sendBroadcast(
        new Intent(
            "xper.receiver.intent.RECEIVER_SEA_AREA_INTENT").
        setFlags(
            Intent.FLAG_RECEIVER_REPLACE_PENDING).
        putExtra(
            "N",
            "One"));
    sendBroadcast(
        new Intent(
            "xper.receiver.intent.RECEIVER_SEA_AREA_INTENT").
        setFlags(
            Intent.FLAG_RECEIVER_REPLACE_PENDING).
        putExtra(
            "N",
            "Two"));
    sendBroadcast(
        new Intent(
            "xper.receiver.intent.RECEIVER_SEA_AREA_INTENT").
        setFlags(
            Intent.FLAG_RECEIVER_REPLACE_PENDING).
        putExtra(
            "N",
```

"Three"));

then we get (output slightly reformatted)

```
Lundy.onReceive(..., Intent { act=xper.receiver.intent.RECEIVER_SEA_AREA_INTENT flg=0x20000000
(has extras) })
Lundy.onReceive(...) N == One

Fastnet.onReceive(..., Intent { act=xper.receiver.intent.RECEIVER_SEA_AREA_INTENT \
  flg=0x20000000 cmp=xper.receiver.fastnet/.Fastnet (has extras) })
Fastnet.onReceive(...) N == One

Lundy.onReceive(..., Intent { act=xper.receiver.intent.RECEIVER_SEA_AREA_INTENT flg=0x20000000
(has extras) })
Lundy.onReceive(...) N == Two

Lundy.onReceive(..., Intent { act=xper.receiver.intent.RECEIVER_SEA_AREA_INTENT flg=0x20000000
(has extras) })
Lundy.onReceive(...) N == Three

Sole.onReceive(..., Intent { act=xper.receiver.intent.RECEIVER_SEA_AREA_INTENT \
  flg=0x20000000 cmp=xper.receiver.sole/.Sole (has extras) })
Sole.onReceive(...) N == One

Fastnet.onReceive(..., Intent { act=xper.receiver.intent.RECEIVER_SEA_AREA_INTENT \
  flg=0x20000000 cmp=xper.receiver.fastnet/.Fastnet (has extras) })
Fastnet.onReceive(...) N == Three

Sole.onReceive(..., Intent { act=xper.receiver.intent.RECEIVER_SEA_AREA_INTENT \
  flg=0x20000000 cmp=xper.receiver.sole/.Sole (has extras) })
Sole.onReceive(...) N == Three
```

11. Sending A Broadcast Intent To A Specific BroadcastReceiver

Both normal and ordered broadcast Intents can be sent to a specific BroadcastReceiver by setting the broadcast
Intent's component explicitly.

For example, assuming the Application package is

    xper.specific

and the BroadcastReceiver is declared as follows

```
<receiver
  android:name = "SpecificBroadcastReceiver">
  <intent-filter>
    <action android:name = "xper.specific.SPECIFIC_BROADCAST_INTENT"/>
  </intent-filter>
```

```
</receiver>
```

then a normal broadcast Intent can be sent to it as follows.

```
sendBroadcast(
    new Intent(
        "xper.specific.BROADCAST_INTENT").
    setClassName(
        "xper.specific",
        "xper.specific.SpecificBroadcastReceiver"));
```

Note that, as in this example, the Intent **does not** have to match the IntentFilter(s) associated with the BroadcastReceiver, which has some interesting implications.

Although specifying the BroadcastReceiver explicitly when sending the broadcast Intent overrides the BroadcastReceiver's IntentFilter(s) both sender and/or receiver permissions, if specified, still apply.

It is not possible to send a broadcast Intent to a specific BroadcastReceiver in sticky mode. Attempting to do so results in a SecurityException.

12. Anonymous BroadcastReceivers

It is possible to statically register a BroadcastReceiver without any IntentFilters. For example.

```
<receiver
    android:name = "AnonymousBroadcastReceiver"/>
```

Broadcast Intents can still be sent to it by specifying the BroadcastReceiver explicitly.

In this can it can only be done from the registering Application since in the BroadcastReceiver has not been exported.

It is of course possible to export it as well

```
<receiver
    android:name    = "AnonymousBroadcastReceiver"
    android:exported = "true"/>
```